only one Angel

Also by Jan Kemp:

Against the Softness of Woman (1976)
Diamonds and Gravel (1979)
Ice-breaker Poems (pamphlet, 1980)
Five Poems (pamphlet, 1988)
The Other Hemisphere (1991)
The Sky's Enormous Jug (2001)

only one angel

poems by
Jan Kemp

OTAGO

Published by University of Otago Press
PO Box 56/56 Union Street, Dunedin, New Zealand
Fax: 64 3 479 8385. Email: university.press@otago.ac.nz

First published 2001
Copyright © Jan Kemp 2001
ISBN 1877276 17 0

Published with the assistance of Creative New Zealand

Cover and text design by Anneloes Douglas
Printed in New Zealand by Printlink Ltd, Wellington

acknowledgements

Very special thanks to Claudia Pond Eyley
for her cover drawings and illustrations
on pages 15, 27 and 48.

Thanks to *Antipodes, Hecate, JAAM, NZ Books,
Poetry New Zealand* and *The Poetic Voice*
(University of Salzburg), where some of
these poems first appeared.

preface

Poets are more likely to gain reputations – to be read, talked about, and appreciated – when they belong to an identifiable 'scene'. Once well-known as the sole woman anthologised in *The Young New Zealand Poets* (1973) and co-star with Hone Tuwhare, Alistair Campbell, and Sam Hunt on a national poetry-reading tour (1979), Jan Kemp has spent decades overseas, while numerous other gifted women writers have claimed our attention. But Kemp, though absent, has not been silent, and now she is back. *Only One Angel* shows the maturing of a highly original talent. New Zealand poetry is the richer for this volume.

It bears the evidence of her travels. She rides an elephant in New Delhi, drives along the Via Saleria 'towards' the Roman poets Poppaia and Orazio, turns off the Austrian Autobahn down a two-way road into Bohemia, descends the rocky Chemin des Serres de la Madone 'a few bays round the coast' from Nietzsche's 'precipitous Zarathustrian / speaking-tongued cliffs at Eze', explores Frankfurt's cathedral, touches the hand of the Black Madonna at Montserrat, ruminates on Giordano Bruno's statue in Rome's Campo de' Fiori where he was burned at the stake for heresy. Places stir associations, are peopled with the dead as well as the living. In the Musée Préhistorique even 'Menton Man' speaks across the millennia: 'You can hear his words after storms / tossed up onto the beach as stones'. Poems are sparked by snippets of information about Verdi, Salvador Dali, or Goethe, pay homage to Hildegard of Bingen, celebrate Caravaggio's 'Ragazzo con frutta', or enter the world of Aboriginal painter Emlly Kame Kngwarreye. The selection is framed by two angel poems 'for' Rilke. 'Only One Angel' challenges his assertion in the first of his *Duino Elegies* that 'all angels are terrible', finding that one with a human face and the power to comfort is 'enough'. But 'The Terrible Angel' is also real, a necessary source of inspiration.

Jan Kemp's lyricism is strengthened by close acquaintance with loss and death. There are beautiful elegiac pieces about her father and mother. But the range of tones is broad, including the witty, the whimsical, and the playful. 'The Ballad of Donna Quixote' gives a feminine slant on Cervantes' novel. The poet also takes on the guise of 'Ms

Quasimodo'. Noah's wife's point of view is expressed in a 'Song'.

Keats wrote of the poet's identifying with a sparrow pecking in the gravel. Kemp has that sort of empathy. She looks closely at things, as well as people, and coaxes them to yield up their secrets. She relishes the quirkiness of language, the sounds of words and the patterns they form, the way they chime and echo. These are poems for the ear, not just the eye. Two are about learning German. In 'Snow or alles ist klar' thoughts about the phenomenon and thoughts about 'studying Deutsch' dissolve into one another. In the next poem the speaker is 'Teetering on the brink of fluency / like someone on a uni-cycle': the simile is carried through with theatrical flair. 'Truth' returns us to 'gritty anglo-saxon words', needed when the 'heart is fallow'.

But the heart has its seasons. In 'Wedding / Naming / Bells' the poet, about to marry, confronts a feminist dilemma. She speculates about going 'to the end of the alphabet / from the middle, when my name's called' or having 'a double-banger', contrasts Chinese custom, and then imagines husband's and wife's surnames as gifts to the other, carrying the mana of 'illustrious ancestors' – in Dieter's case the German medieval sculptor Tilman Riemenschneider, in Jan's case Shakespeare's popular fellow-actor Will Kempe, who 'in 1600 danced a jig / all the way in jingling bells / from London to Norwich'. It is a warm and loving poem, typical in its lightness of touch and the play of fancy that leads to those exotic wedding bells. Jan Kemp knows that 'naming' gives our lives meaning, constructs our world; that words can dance, perform, celebrate. Her poems are gifts that we can all share.

Mac Jackson
Auckland 2001

to my husband pieter
and to the memory
of my mother
Joan Anne (née Hooten) Kemp
23 May 1920-29 August 2001

only one angel

for Rainer Maria Rilke

Not all angels are terrible.
One's
here
for me.
Only she
(or he).

Every time
I fall on my knee
only he
(or she).

Every time
I land
on the ground
only she/he's around.

It's enough.
One angel's enough.

The Ballad
of Donna Quixote

I want to be
a Viennese lady
eating up Art in a cloche.

I want to walk
down the Champs Élysées
with a husband who drives in a Porsche.

I want to be posh & benign
at the very same time
& to survive entirely on spinach —

but I'm Donna Quixote
so as likely as not
my dreams are all there is in it.

* *

My Sancha Panzetta
my faithful my friend
she's round she's short & she's homely —

she'll never leave me
alone in the lurch
nor will my car, Rosinante.

I want to propose
with the tip of my nose
to my gallant my handsome Don Duce —
but I've learned like a wallflower
to wait in the wings
till his stirrups spur him

to send me a rose
to tell me I'm comely
to say I'm his only.

* *

And in the meantime...

* *

I want to know love
like the back of my palm
I want regents and rajahs to woo me —

to have portraits by painters
of numberless charm.
I want Cleopatra to sue me.

I want to float down the Nile
in my very own barge
whose oarsmen make off with my booty —

I want to be loved
by the man in the moon
who'll say simply, *my Donna, my Beauty.*

* *

I want to know poets
to speak in their tongues
& converse with the mighty & learned.

I want to move mountains
all on my own & if lost
be found by Saint Bernard.

* *

I want to have style
elan & pizzazz.
I want to be kind

most refined
non-aligned.
I want to be mother of millions.

I want wandering souls
to find rest in my tent.
I want them to say

I'm better, Ms Quixote
for your tea and biscuit —
you're sort of a Florence

though without a lamp —
thanks very much
for my time in your camp.

* *

I want to live life.
I want to be raucous & wild
or demure and most mild —

but I'm Donna Quixote
& my dreams are
all windmills and tulips.

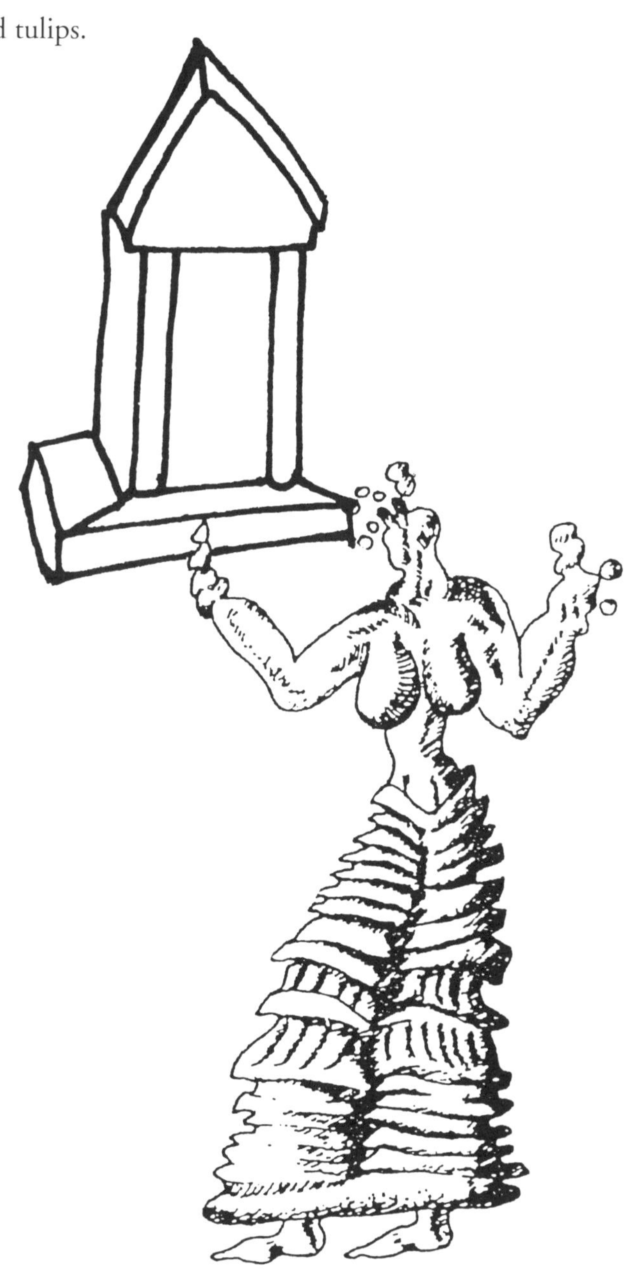

ᴍѕ Quasimodo

I wish you'd phone up now
so you'd know
how like a crone I live.

I wish you'd phone up now
so you'd find me huddled over my rice
& some book or other.

I think of you constantly
& constantly put you out of mind —
a turned page, an empty bowl.

When I hobble away from the table
I wish you'd see the beady eyes on either side
of my huge damp red promontory.

But no one calls. I'll go & swing on the bells.

Mistress Rose

To have been loved by so many
yet belong to none. Starkly realising
the gardener she thought would tend her
was a trick of light that fell only in season

she closed her petals one by one
& turned the tightened buds into words
of an unbewildered truth — to flower
belonging only to the garden & herself.

LOTUS

*Verdi was particularly attached to the 'Te Deum'
from his* Quattro Pezzi Sacri *& is said
to have wished it to be buried with him.*

The lotus lifts herself out of the mud.
She sings for love.

Keep with you what you would be buried with
if there, in the middle of a note
you were to die
in a choir of voices.

seventh floor, flat A

A little drama she enacts
pottering about in it
making tea to keep accord
as a woman with facilities
in a home might, alone, insomniac
in the middle of the night.

Not much to do, write
an odd sort of letter
eat a water-biscuit
read a few words.

Does she get caught up
in the eddies of memory
forget how to fight her way
back to the present?
Does she drown?
Happily?

They say, if you listen
to the silence
from the bottom of a pond
the noises in your ears
will splash about
like floundering thrushes.

Truth

Only you
gritty anglo-saxon words
can answer me
when my heart is fallow when
it touches my backbone.

I shall take you off my tongue
the bits of self-delusion
I cannot swallow
& put you on the page
& look at you.

My Heart is a columbarium

There aren't many corners
of it left to tuck you away in
waiting for a cure

for circumstantial parting.
My heart is a handkerchief
of knotted corners.

When I look at the full moon
I must try to remember
who's where. And now you

my brightest luminary, want to
lock us up too, in the meantime
'living as if we'll never meet again'

but preserving the ashes
in the hope one day together
we'll scatter them on the sea

under the real true moon
that will put all others
in the shade. *Yes,* I say

more faintly this time, much less
sure of romance, certain of reality
I'll keep a corner for you.

when

When they were like that she loved him
playing child to child no masks
and even in his Arabian net
of form & ostentation, duty & will.

When the air touched their faces
as they lay and he said
*feel the little wind — we don't
have much but we have that.*

wave

Until I heard your voice
I had hidden the ocean
in my heart.

Now my resolution
rages on the beach
my longing echoes down the coast to Kapiti.

pilgrims

For each of us — so many moments alive.
She couldn't see then through his eyes
the year only he could give — an apricot season
spread on the tree of the present.
She wanted a normal life
not to have to return
to the hard road of the pilgrim.

The orchard now picked clean
she is constant & tireless
as are the moon the stars
or the stones on that road.

rain

The night you flew away
it rained
soft rain
to veil your going
rain which knows you'll return.

I'll be there
on the other side of the glass
in your reflection
when you look for me
in this slipping world.

song of Noah's wife

on seeing a medieval wood-cut:
'Noah's wife at his ship with her two gossips'

You are my Noah
yet I will not mask
love's face with yours
for you are love's
face, not love.

I may bring my gossips
with me to your ship, like girls
giggling behind our hands
but we are neither girls nor gossips.
Yet gossips & girls

are to us as is love's face
to you. Know this, Noah —
whatever shape it takes
your sons, Ham, Shem & Japheth,
the animals, the peace to come

after war's flood, who knows what:
what dissembles is flower not seed
resembles is seed not flower —
for when I looked again
I saw love at last, not love's face.

in Karlskirche

That pain again
losing a country
or a friend. What nowhere
have they
fallen into?

I can only
turn to new love,
who sits with me
in the soundless well
of Karlskirche.

frankfurter dom

Frankfurt's cathedral is full of ships.
Quite a port. Nordschiff, Südschiff
Hauptschiff A, B, C, D,
not to mention the High Choir.

The only shape
left afloat in WWII
hurtling up out of the rubble
the Dom sang out
a siren
in a sea of bombs.

The rose-stone Dom
where Goethe's father's
painter friends & gentlefolk
once walked
in the light falling
amidships
from Gothic windows
talking.

ship

As a swimmer
dreaming idly
on the ocean's belly
suddenly
a ship
my 3-masted schooner
you'd sent
over the horizon.

Icarus should
have been
so lucky & set off too
in a new direction
full of cumulus & wonder
at the string-tuggings
of love & Jupiter
who, astrologers say,
always pulls you
to the right
location.

'one loses privacy with a woman in love'

What would you wish
privacy or love —
sanctity or what
the saints reprove.

Twice happy love that
sanctifies as it proves
privacy shared
is doubly loved.

Should we refuse
her dance, love
would have us saints
& we be lost.

wedding / naming / bells

When I marry you I'll go
to the end of the alphabet
from the middle, when my name's called

or if I stand in alphabeticised queues.

I'll have a double-banger
as you do in Europe:
Frau Such-and-such hyphen Such-and-such.

In China or Hong Kong
I'd just be Madame Mee
& you'd be Sir Yu.
No one would know
of our connection
unless they knew.

Now, I'll be Madame Yu-hyphen-Mee
& you'll still be Sir Yu
(unless of course in case
you take my name too)
when you'd be Sir Mee-Yu

but would we then belong?
We'd be in different places
in the queue. Anyway, your
name's so long you hardly
need my short one.

But otherwise
it could be nice
to pretend allegiance to
our illustrious ancestors

to whom connection
through the loss of documents
& manuscripts from
    wars
    famine
    burning
    history's catastrophes
    who knows what
is almost completely wiped out
except for our names.

So, you could say
when you marry me —

I hand on my lovely name
meaning 'cutter-of-belts'
which Tilman Riemenschneider, sculptor
fifteenth century, Rothenburg & such
long sad fine face & fingers, wore

to you.
And I could say —
I hand on mine, Middle English, 'champion'
at that time 'champion wrestler',
which Will wore, our Will Kempe
who well knew the other oh-so-famous Bill
& in 1600 danced a jig

all the way in jingling bells
from London to Norwich.

And then, that said
would we be wed?

snow or
Alles ist klar (studying deutsch)

I
Snow lies in the dative case
on the roof *(auf dem Dach)*
     DATIV.
I go out into
the snowstrewn street *(in die Strasse)*
     AKKUSATIV
quite unaccusingly
thinking which preposition
takes what
depends on how you feel —

Germans like it to be all
tied linguistically neatly down
(zu etwas tied-down sein)
FUNKTIONSVERB

to know where one is
(in the whiteness of snow).

II
The next day it has
all completely disappeared
— *verschwunden* —
no *PREPOSITION.*
(Could I say this
in the passive voice?)
     PASSIV?

By going out actively
in the snow
perhaps the accumulation
of human breathings-out
dissolves it
as if it
never even was?

But to tell you the truth
I saw that gone snow on the roof.

Now it lies only
in meinem Kopf (in my head)
DATIV.

The Brink of Fluency

Teetering on the brink of fluency
like someone on a uni-cycle
I fall suddenly
plötzlich
a mosquito
squashed again
by the *allmächtige* almighty Hand
of German Grammar
a black etching
on red smudge
tyres quite burst

einatmen
ausatmen
breathe in
breathe out
I say to myself
meditatively
gazing up
at the uni-cycle's
precarious pedals
freewheeling above me
like verbs or nouns
trennbar oder zusammengesetzt
separable or not
I don't care much which
as I lie
on the *Fussboden*
ground
still gazing up

wondering
how many *Fehler* (failures) will still fall
feathers to fell
my yet-again stride?

I climb up
brush *selbst* self down
set teeth on edge
grit my ears, shout —

Wait, Rilke! Elke Laske Schüler!
Ingeborg Bachmann! Günter Grass!
I'm just coming round the corner
wait for me!

As Goethe said —
Warte nur, balde
verstehest Du auch.
(just wait, soon you'll get it).

Bohemian Road

The traffic of Bohemia
follows one two-way road
from the Austrian *Autobahn*
through forest & villages.

Over empty
winter fields
where woodcutters' ghosts
walk abroad

night enters
the bus window
wide & spreading
from a falling moon

& treads
on our hands
held under your coat
for warmth

beneath the vaultings
of life we enter into
this unknown road
new country.

chemin des serres de la madone, menton

At last I've found
my path of the Madonna's greenhouses —

Papa Earth Mother Magnificat
wriggling all the way down a corniche

where mesculin, lavender & thyme grow wild
a few bays round the coast

from Nietzsche's precipitous Zarathustrian
speaking-tongued cliffs at Eze.

Did that peripatetic philosopher
know he had the lot of us

coming after him
shouting our poems

from rocky paths
inching down to the sea?

flag

for Hildegard of Bingen

How high
a regard
you can hold
when it flaps
holistic: potions & prayers
diademed nuns
herbs, beer & rabbits
most altruistic.

Apart from the music
what I love best
is the woodcut —
the flames on her head
Volmar the scribe
at slate & chalk
& the talk
through the portal
like pearls.

Emily Kame Kngwarreye

born c. 1910 Alhalkere, Utopia, Northern Territory
died 2 September 1996, Alice Springs, Northern Territory

Whole lot
I paint whole lot
she laughs
paints grasses
yellow-green
swirling
windy dry
huge
coloured
tangles
all the way
to red
4000
paintings
eight years
jump off canvasses
titled
untitled
bold white on black
thick
yam patch
dreaming
8 metres by 3
cracked earth
parched
patterns
bird's-eye Australia

22 *fauve*
broken panel
greens to mauve
bush to sunset
waterfalls
coloured squiggles
bodyribs
skeletons
scratchy red
& brown
gold
yellow
brush tip splodges
summer
whole lot
shouts
buoyant big being
signature:
Emlly

Elephant Riding

Climbing up
the back of an elephant
you spring into
the toehold of its tail
held in place by the mahout
grab the ropes
strapped round its belly
& haul yourself up.

She rises
from buckled knees under you
moves like a ship
you're high
under the hanging ashoka leaves
as you flow forward
her fly-bitten ears grey sails flap.
She flings the odd young-leaved branch
into her mouth
with her triumphant trunk.

You want to scratch
the top of her stubbled head
tell her it's like riding a whale
they're both your favourite creatures
you'd like to know their languages
couldn't she speak
just a little of hers?

But the mahout down on the road
rubs thumb & finger together

furiously you nod
yes pay, of course we'll pay
thinking, if he doesn't
accept our offer, let me down
I'll be stuck up here forever
riding New Delhi streets
with the mahout's boy
or it'll suddenly have had enough
trumpet & fling me off or bolt.

I'd never have paid
till he let you down
you said, as we watched her
join the diesel-belching traffic circle
my ship of the jungle
dirty & grey
non-caparisoned, gentle, knowing, female
working animal.

In India, they say
a woman is beautiful
when she walks
like an elephant.

# 'Ragazzo con frutta'

after Caravaggio

In my bed the same
lidded eyes feed me
grapes with every
undercover look — his
name painted as signature
on fruit & curly head.

I think the painter
a pagan prince
love's musician
got into the picture
three hundred years back.

Volcanic in nature
like you he is all
light and shadow
on the pillows
light bursting

from under hooded lids
or strumming fingers —
his silk shirt
spilling like lava
off his back & the bed
a wine-press.

gold ring

Did this gold ring I wear
come from Cairo with my father
to mother's finger, binding
her troth after the war

forty-two years, until rheumatic
knuckles stopped the wearing
& he went to the Egypt of hereafter
swaddled in the love of children, wife.

Again he plays piano within cooee
of the Pyramids, an ear attuned
to the golden oldies, an eye winking
into the surveyor's periscope

in the Western desert. Forever
smiling, Rommel forgotten, he lies asleep
after Xmas dinner '42 in a tent.
The sepia photos I found in his trunk

locking my dolls away in khaki blankets
go browner now. From these
my first glimpse of Giza
like some Egyptian child's, perhaps

of a New Zealand soldier on leave
whose unborn daughter's mother's
fine, new wedding ring
she watched him buy in a Maadi market.

centuries

They've always seemed so far
but they're not —
Poppaia & Orazio as close now
as Via Salaria

we drove down yesterday
straight as a gannet
diving
between twinned lindens —

the salt road
built 361 BC
& we're on it
still, now & into
the never-never!

Any century you choose
just visit. Take an
etruscan vase
for instance
by the handles —
(watch out for
the museum attendant)

pluck basil
pull carrots
from the Marches —
'O Italy'
as Leopardi said
(unified now again)

your fecundity's
a cornucopic barrowful
wheeled up from the garden
below sloping vines
by Enrico, neighbouring —

just take
paintings, figs, crypts
tomatoes, plums, mosaics
he said
what you want!

queen of the castle

I
My mother had the right idea
a hairclip high on either side
& drawn back from the part —
me in braces smiling in a pinafore.

I am a Duchess
licking un-lipsticked lips
carrying keys in a wicker basket
to unlock the castle.

Children sing to me in the courtyard.
I stand on the steps in
a down-at-heel costume (bone
buttons, turned-back linen lapels)

ready with my Marlene Dietrich
glamour hairstyle to show them
the rusting armour & coats-of-arms
our family is so proud of.

O to be a last Duchess & show
children the mysteries
my mother dreamed of
Europe's histories.

She, the girl in fairy wings
carrying a silver-starred wand
in 'Party, Xmas Eve', about 1930
Harry Linley Richardson

who stood in tableaux at school
in wispy garments & headband
being photographed balancing —
who signed her Still Lives

at Art Class simply J.A.
in careful coloured pencil
with shading & perspective
a pear, an apple, a peach

our mother, Joan Anne
at 80, just out of reach
whose speech
repeats & repeats

Darling, how lovely, darling how …
I wish I wish …
swish swish swish …
each word as new as the one before.

II
On the drawing room's window sill
the antique vase's chandelier crystals
make rainbows on the frosted panes
while I practise to the metronome.

Notes float through the house
to her preparing breakfasts. *Darling*
how well you … & as my arpeggios stagger
Oh dear, don't stop, try again. I'm here.

the silence

Go on listening to the silence
which holds all sound
till the last cricket tricks you
into thinking it has no wings.

Benisons of white gulls
fall from the lips of silence.
Her eyes are open & closed.
She is breathing.

Do not disturb her.

At her own Hearth

for Anna & Diana Justice

The dead speak
another idiom, pure
contra/diction.
The eyelids of roses
please them, as they
float through
pale & seeing
as light growing
accustomed to day.

Two converse.
I was a leaf once
on a Japanese tree
then a blue scarab
beetle. And you?
 I? A strong peasant
woman. I held on long
though two years blind
& since my stroke
trapped in my body's skirts.

I see my daughters now
sitting shiva
speaking again
freed of old hurts.
It is most pleasing.
One needs only
to go through. Here too
I am at my own hearth.

'full fathom five'

Musée Préhistorique, Menton

Menton Man
lies folding himself
to the left
in his skeleton sepulchre —

25,000 years BC
he died at forty
his skull a cap
of cockle-shells & stag's spit
faintly apricot & cream.

You can hear his words after storms
tossed up onto the beach as stones.

spanish eyes

Found in Te Papa, March 2000:
*'IN TRUTH, in very truth a grain of wheat I tell you now, remains a solitary grain
/ unless it falls into the ground and DIES / but if it dies it becomes a rich harvest.'*
A grain of wheat Feb 1970 Muriwai, Colin McCahon

I
This sprig of Spring I keep
this *blé*
this heart of wheat
this maize
this *spighe*
this ear
through which I hear
'the golden Hand
the infinite' (Miro)
the sun

holds
the bread of day
in a basket
panier
cesta del pan
woven from cane.

II
One loaf we share
& broken fishes
swimming away —
their tails
busy fins

the sea
can hardly contain
their spines
like this wheat's
with flesh gone —
a rounded cross
with ladder bones.

III
To telephone to God
Dali placed
six mirrors
in a silver briefcase
with phonesets
either side.
Are you there?
Hola?
Hello?

IV
Gala Looking At the Mediterranean

Gala's freedom
is to look
at the Mediterranean
is she
not
there?
It's light.
It's Abraham Lincoln's
portrait

pequeño y grande
both portrayed.
It's 'is and isn't'.

VI
In the museum
at Figuéras
a shower in a Cadillac!

VII
Sprigs full of life's wheat —
light of Spanish ochre
over the Pyrenees —
I thought the world
was through my eyes
until I saw it.

VIII
What we see
changes / wakes us
up to the facts. Art is
a self-portrait. What
I say I've seen.

IX
I've been to Spain
drunk *Jaume* wine
touched the hand
of the Black Madonna
at Montserrat — mine
fell off hers onto
the universe she holds.

I asked for a natural life
(you're supposed to wish)
that is to say: I want
to live including death.

The Terrible Angel

for Rainer Maria Rilke

Don't leave off speaking to the wind
though your voice will block me deaf
nor stop setting down the light
though your eyes will shut me.
The elements are yours are mine
& we are marked by likeness.
Angel, recognise my face!

Alphabetical list of titles